The AMERICAN REVOLUTION

1763 – 1783

The AMERICAN REVOLUTION

1763 –1783

Christopher Collier
James Lincoln Collier

BENCHMARK BOOKS

MARSHALL CAVENDISH
NEW YORK

ACKNOWLEDGMENT: The authors wish to thank Richard D. Brown, Professor of History, University of Connecticut, for his careful reading of the text of this volume of The Drama of American History, and his thoughtful and useful comments. The work has been much improved by Professor Dowd's notes. The authors are deeply in his debt but, of course, assume full responsibility for the substance of the work, including any errors that may appear.

Photo research by James Lincoln Collier
COVER PHOTO: *The Metropolitan Museum of Art,* Gift of John Stewart Kennedy, 1897. (97.34). Photograph © 1992 *The Metropolitan Museum of Art.*
PICTURE CREDITS: The photographs in this book are used by permission and through the courtesy of: *Corbis-Bettmann:* 11, 17, 26, 28, 34, 37 (right), 39, 43, 46, 49, 56, 58, 63 (top), 65, 77. *Colonial Williamsburg Foundation:* 14, 15, 16, 18, 19, 25, 27, 31, 33, 37 (left), 40, 41, 80, 85. *Jamestown-Yorktown Educational Trust:* 52 (top), 52 (bottom), 81. *The Metropolitan Museum of Art,* Gift of John Stewart Kennedy, 1897; (97.34); photograph © 1992 *The Metropolitan Museum of Art:* 70. *Abby Aldrich Rockefeller Folk Art Center, Williamsburg, Virginia:* 63 (bottom).

AUTHORS' NOTE: The human beings who first peopled what we now call the Americas have traditionally been called *Indians,* because the first Europeans who landed in the Americas thought they had reached India. The term *Indians* is therefore not very accurate, and other terms have been used: *Amerinds,* and more recently, *Native Americans.* The Indians had no collective term for themselves. Today, most of them refer to themselves as Indians, and we will use that term here, while understanding that it is not very accurate.

Benchmark Books
Marshall Cavendish Corporation
99 White Plains Road
Tarrytown, New York 10591-9001

© 1998 Christopher Collier and James Lincoln Collier

Library of Congress Cataloging-in-Publication Data

Collier, Christopher, date
The American Revolution /
Christopher Collier, James Lincoln Collier.
p.   cm.
Includes bibliographical references and index.
ISBN 0-7614-0440-6 (lib. bdg.)
1. United States—History—Revolution, 1763–1783—Juvenile literature.
[1. United States—History—Revolution, 1763–1783.]
I. Collier, James Lincoln, date. II. Title. III. Series.
E208.C66   96-45440
973.3—dc21 1997   CIP
                                                                                        AC
Printed in the United States of America

1 3 5 6 4 2

CONTENTS

Over many years of both teaching and writing for students at all levels, from grammar school to graduate school, it has been borne in on us that many, if not most, American history textbooks suffer from trying to include everything of any moment in the history of the nation. Students become lost in a swamp of factual information, and as a consequence lose track of how those facts fit together, and why they are significant and relevant to the world today.

In this series, our effort has been to strip the vast amount of available detail down to a central core. Our aim is to draw in bold strokes, providing enough information, but no more than is necessary, to bring out the basic themes of the American story, and what they mean to us now. We believe that it is surely more important for students to grasp the underlying concepts and ideas that emerge from the movement of history than to memorize an array of facts and figures.

The difference between this series and many standard texts lies in what has been left out. We are convinced that students will better remember the important themes if they are not buried under a heap of names, dates, and places.

In this sense, our primary goal is what might be called citizenship education. We think it is critically important for America as a nation and Americans as individuals to understand the origins and workings of the public institutions which are central to American society. We have asked ourselves again and again what is most important for citizens of our democracy to know so they can most effectively make the system work for them and the nation. For this reason, we have focused on political and institutional history, leaving social and cultural history less well developed.

This series is divided into volumes that move chronologically through the American story. Each is built around a single topic, such as the pilgrims, the Constitutional Convention, or immigration. Each volume has been written so that it can stand alone, for students who wish to research a given topic. As a consequence, in many cases material from previous volumes is repeated, usually in abbreviated form, to set the topic in its historical context. That is to say, students of the Constitutional Convention must be given some idea of relations with England, and why the revolution was fought, even though the material was covered in detail in a previous volume. Readers should find that each volume tells an entire story that can be read with or without reference to other volumes.

Despite our belief that it is of the first importance to outline sharply basic concepts and generalizations, we have not neglected the great dramas of American history. The stories that will hold the attention of students are here, and we believe they will help the concepts they illustrate to stick in their minds. We think, for example, that knowing of Abraham Baldwin's brave and dramatic decision to vote with the small states at the Constitutional Convention will bring alive the Connecticut Compromise, out of which grew the American Senate.

Each of these volumes has been read by esteemed specialists in its particular topic; we have benefited from their comments.

CHAPTER I

A Revolution in the Hearts and Minds of Americans

The biggest puzzle about the American Revolution, one of the most important events of the modern age, is whether it had to happen at all. Was it inevitable? Couldn't leaders on both sides, most of them intelligent, educated, thoughtful people, have found a way around it? After all, only these thirteen of Britain's some thirty-odd colonies in the New World chose to break with England. To this day nations like Canada, the Cayman Islands, and some of the Virgin Islands in the Caribbean are still loosely joined to what remains of the British Empire. But the thirteen colonies from Georgia through New Hampshire on the Atlantic Coast of North America chose to fight for their independence from England, and thus brought into being the nation whose history we are studying, the United States of America.

To understand what happened, we need to know what people on *both* sides of the Atlantic Ocean were thinking. For behind what people *do* is not only what they feel but also what they *think*—how they see the world, what they believe is right and wrong. Taking both head and heart into account, John Adams, who was deeply involved in the events leading up to the war between the English and Americans, claimed that the real American Revolution began with a "radical change in the principles, opinions, sentiments, and affections of the people." That is to say, before the 1760s, Americans thought one way about their relations to the mother country, England; afterward they began to think another way about it. And the new way of thinking led them, step by step, into an insoluble conflict with the English.

But of course what the English in England thought about America and the Americans mattered, too. If either—or both—side had been able to adjust its thinking in the years before 1775, there might not have been an American Revolution, and the history of recent centuries would have been quite different. Let us begin by looking at the situation through British eyes.

The English colonies in North America had been established haphazardly—in a "fit of absentmindedness," as one historian put it. The rulers in London did not, until long after the colonies were well established, attempt to organize them into a single system. Various kings and queens gave grants of huge tracts of land—some of them reaching from the Atlantic to the Pacific—not only to their friends and creditors, but also to adventurers, explorers, stock companies of merchants, and investors. Many of the people involved, both the monarchs and the investors, had only a hazy understanding of American geography, so that more than once the same territory was given to two different people. Complicating matters, other European nations, especially France, Holland, and Spain, were claiming some of the same land.

Inevitably, at least at first, each colony had its own type of government. Some—the so-called proprietary colonies—were each owned lock, stock, and barrel by one wealthy Englishman, who could pretty much do as he pleased with the colony, provided he followed the laws of England. Others were ruled by stock companies, who put in their own governors. Some—the royal colonies—were controlled directly by whoever was on the throne of England at the time. Still others—called charter colonies—

This famous cartoon, designed by Benjamin Franklin, pronounced what would be the key theme in America for a third of a century, from the French and Indian War beginning in 1754, when the cartoon was printed, to the ratification of the Constitution in 1789, when the states were finally unified. Through those thirty-five years the great question was: Could the colonies ever pull together?

like Massachusetts and Connecticut, in the main elected their own governments. On top of it, all of the revolutionary colonies in time established elected legislatures, which had a certain degree of say in things.

There were several reasons why the English established these colonies in such a haphazard fashion. For one thing, during the period in question, roughly through the 1600s, England itself was extremely unsettled and changing. Parliament and the kings were jostling for power. Puritans, Catholics, Anglicans, Quakers, and other religious sects were contending for the hearts and minds of the English people. Unemployment was widespread. In the struggle one king was beheaded in 1649. The government that followed collapsed in 1660 and a new king was brought in. His successor lasted only for three years, and in 1689, yet another new king arrived. Thus when the American colonies were being founded the English were much taken up with events at home and paid less attention to what was going on across the Atlantic than they should have.

Another reason why the American colonies were settled so unsystematically had to do with the way the English thought about them. Everybody concerned saw them mainly for the quick profits that might be taken out of them. The kings of the time were always getting themselves into small wars with their neighbors, and needed money for troops and supplies. They wanted to see flowing across the Atlantic a steady stream of furs, fish, tobacco, timber, and other products, which would bring profits to the English merchants and revenue to the king. The investors put a lot of money into their own colonies, sometimes their whole fortunes, and were eager to see some of that money coming back. Ordinary people wanted the colonies to create jobs back home—jobs for sailors plying the Atlantic trade, for shipbuilders, for hat-makers who used the beaver fur to make felt, for sellers of tobacco. In a word, the English saw the American colonies as being there for the good of *England*. As long as the money rolled in, the English tended to let the Americans go about things their own way.

At first the colonies accepted the idea that they belonged to England. They believed they were English men and women, that the colonies were extensions of England, and they tried, as much as they could, to create in America the English way of life.

As English people, they expected to have the rights that traditionally or by law belonged to the people back home—for example, the right to trial by jury, the right to petition the government for redress of their grievances, and more. But they also believed that the king had rights, too. This was a time when nearly everybody accepted the idea that God had intended some people to rule and some to follow, and they did not object to the king and Parliament enacting laws that would benefit England more than the colonies. That was, as most people saw it, the natural order of things.

But there was an important difference that made Americans think just a little bit differently about themselves and their government from the way the people from back home thought. England was a small island nation, where people, goods, news, and ideas could spread quickly around the country. The American colonies, on the other hand, were weeks, even months, away from London. It might be six months before news of an event in America reached England, and another six months before an order in response got back to the colonies. As a consequence, everybody recognized that the colonists had to be able to settle certain matters among themselves, and as the colonies came into being each set up some sort of legislature, elected by men with varied but always specified amounts of property. It was understood, however, that in most cases the king, or his governor in the colony, could overturn laws passed by these legislatures.

But in fact, that was not so easy for a king or a governor to do. The only way a king could enforce his rulings was to send a lot of troops into each colony to make people do what he wanted. This would be very expensive, and would take the profit out of the colonies. In the end, the rulers of England tended to leave the colonists alone. If the colonists kept buying English goods and sending to England all of those fish, furs, and the rest of it that would produce a profit for the investors, the mighty in England would let them do as they liked in most other matters. Parliament established various laws to see that money kept coming in. The most important of these said that goods entering England would be subject to an import duty. But this law would not be much use if the colonists sold their goods elsewhere, so a second law was enacted saying that most American products must be shipped directly to England, even though the colonists might get a better price for them in Holland, France, or the Caribbean Islands. This way, not only was the king able to tax the goods, but the merchant investors in England could sell the fish, fur, or whatever to Holland or France, and themselves make the profit. Because they were involved in foreign and civil wars during much of the century after 1640, the English could enforce these laws only sporadically despite their mighty navy. The Americans grumbled about the regulations and got around them when they could—which was often—but for the most part they accepted them in principle.

Through the 1600s and into the 1700s the colonies prospered. The land was fertile, the forests full of game, the waters rich with fish. Many rivers made it easy to carry people and goods in and out of the interior areas. Tens of thousands of Europeans, often living very hard lives in the Old World, poured in. The countryside was cleared and planted in corn,

This reenactment in the restored town of Colonial Williamsburg, once the capital of Virginia, shows a wealthy lady being fitted for a dress. By the time of the Revolution, white Americans were probably better off on average than any people anywhere.

Ordinary people were well able to enjoy life in America, as this reenactment of a tavern scene suggests.

wheat, rice, and many other products. Backwoodsmen traded with the Indians for furs, loggers cut the seemingly endless oak, pine, or cypress trees. Fishermen pulled millions of cod and other fish from the Atlantic each year. Coastal villages, enriched by the products flowing through them, grew into larger and larger towns where wealthy merchants built large houses and filled them with luxuries like gilt mirrors, silver dishes, and cut-glass chandeliers. By the middle of the 1700s North America was a busy, prosperous part of the world. The people, according to one historian, were "by and large, self-confident, resourceful, energetic, and positive, and they displayed a forthrightness born of these qualities."

Inevitably, other European nations had wanted to share in the wealth coming out of America. The Spanish had attempted to colonize the area

The basis of American prosperity was farming: The country shipped huge quantities of farm goods such as wheat, rice, tobacco, and much else to each other and to Europe, the Caribbean, and elsewhere. Oxen were widely used for heavy work, including pulling wagons, and plowing, as in this picture.

around what we now know as Florida, but were never able to make much of it. The Dutch had taken over the lands up and down the Hudson River, and had begun to develop towns—at what are now Albany and New York City. They had not brought many settlers, however, and in the 1600s the English were easily able to conquer the colony. That left only the French, who held what is roughly now Canada, and a chain of forts running down the Mississippi, which gave them some control of the vast interior land between the Appalachian Mountains and the Mississippi.

Other groups of people also claimed the land—the Indians. The human beings who first peopled what we now call the Americas have traditionally been called Indians, because the first Europeans who landed in the Americas thought they had reached India. The term *Indians* is therefore not very accurate, and other terms have been used: *Amerinds,* and more recently, *Native Americans.* The Indians had no term for themselves, as they thought they were all the human beings that there were. Today most of them refer to themselves as Indians, and we will use that term here, while understanding that it is not very accurate

Some of the English settlers saw that the Indians were not being fairly treated, but many were indifferent, and others felt simply that the Indians ought to be driven away. In the end, the invading flood of Europeans cutting down the forests to make farms pressed the Indians farther and farther back. There were battles, massacres on both sides. But

William Penn makes a treaty with the Indians, 1682. In this picture by the celebrated painter Benjamin West, the buildings in the background show how prosperous America had already become. West was born and raised in Pennsylvania, of a Quaker family, but spent most of his career working in England.

Regrettably, a lot of labor was supplied by black slaves, especially in the south. Here two slaves grind corn in a reenactment from Williamsburg.

by the late 1600s the English were in possession of the lands east of the Appalachians.

Now England finally woke up to the fact that it had some extremely valuable possessions along the Atlantic Coast of North America. In 1685, James II became king. He personally held huge pieces of America and had always been interested in the colonies. He started to pull this assortment of colonies into an empire.

However, the Catholic James ran into trouble with the predominantly Protestant Parliament. He was deposed in favor of William of Orange, a Dutchman. The Dutch had built an extremely profitable empire in its colonies, and William understood the value of them more than other kings had. The English began to run the colonies with a tighter rein, systematizing them in ways that they had not done before. And as before, the object was to enrich England; how the colonists came out of it was not much on the minds of the English rulers.

It was clear, however, that the French, established to the north and west, were cutting off English colonies from a vast area of the continent. Especially important was the very profitable fur trade with the Indians in the interior; but land across the Appalachians was also immensely valuable for settlement. For decades these two rivals battled each other in Europe and on the Atlantic Ocean, often involving Americans. In 1754, the focus of the fighting shifted to the New World, in what we now call the French and Indian War. (Readers interested in more detail on this war can consult *The French and Indian War*, the fourth book of this series.) The war began badly for the British, but a crucial victory at Quebec in 1759 turned the tide, and in the Treaty of Paris of 1763 the French ceded what is now Canada to England. England was finally in possession of North America from the Atlantic to the Mississippi River.

Tying the whole system together were the businessmen—shippers and brokers who traded American products for foreign ones, often making themselves wealthy in the process. Here a trader bids on some merchandise.

The character of the colonists of 1763 was different from that of those who had settled the country in the first decades of the 1600s—different even from the people of the 1690s when the English began to systemize their colonial empire. Americans who were old men and women in 1763 when the Treaty of Paris was signed had not even been born when William of Orange came to the English throne in 1689. And they looked back on the pioneers who founded the first English colonies at Jamestown and Plymouth as their dimly perceived ancestors, much as we look back on the people who fought the American Civil War.

Most critically, they *thought* differently from those earlier people— thought differently in ways that, as John Adams said, would amount to the "real American Revolution." What were these new ways of thinking? The first was that the colonists had come to see their legislatures as miniature Parliaments. They quite deliberately adopted Parliamentary procedures in imitation of the one in London. Most significantly, along with Parliamentary practices, they felt they should also have the *powers* of the Parliament.

Like the Americans, Parliament had radically changed. At the time of the first settlements at Jamestown, Virginia, the English king was still paramount over Parliament—or at least was struggling to be so. He, not the members of Parliament, would decide all major issues, especially in regard to the overseas empire. And at the time, a lot of English people believed that was his right.

But in the intervening years the struggle between Parliament and the king had been settled. Parliament had won. In particular, the power to tax now unquestionably belonged to Parliament. Inevitably, all those little parliaments in the colonies concluded that they, too, should have the power to tax.

A second change in the colonists' way of thinking was this. The first settlers had seen themselves as English men and women, and came with the intention of creating, in many respects, a duplicate of England on

American shores. They insisted on calling themselves Englishmen, for one thing so that they might, as we have seen, claim "the rights traditionally accorded Englishmen"—the right to trial by jury and so forth.

By 1763, the colonists no longer thought of themselves as Englishmen in England, but rather as a special kind of Englishmen—*Americans*. Why should they not? In 1763, many American families had been in the country for five generations: there were children growing up in small towns in Massachusetts, Virginia, and elsewhere whose grandfathers' own grandfathers had lived in America.

But the main reason why the colonists had come to think of themselves as Americans was that the English had forced them to that conclusion. Right from the start, the English had seen the colonies as there primarily to do good for the people at home. To them, there had been no other point in undergoing the expense and loss of lives necessary in exploring the new continent, shipping over settlers, fighting off Indians, and supplying the colonies when they got into trouble. That had made a certain amount of sense at the time. The problem was that the English had not changed their way of thinking. They still saw the colonists as serving the interests of England.

In other words, the British government was treating the colonists differently from the way it treated Englishmen in England. The interests of the two peoples were often different, and inevitably, many colonists had come to think of themselves as different, with different ideas, and sometimes conflicting needs.

Americans had begun to think this way some time before 1763. But so long as the French were sitting directly north of them in Canada and had a chain of forts running down the Mississippi by means of which they could control a huge part of the continent, the Americans felt they needed the protection of the powerful British army and the mighty British navy. But now, in 1763, the French threat was gone. The Americans no longer needed the British. The two societies were on a collision course.

CHAPTER II

The Stamp Act Crisis

There now began a series of incidents that gradually wound up the tension between the Americans and the British. The first of these was caused by what is known as the Writs of Assistance. The background to it is this:

As we have seen, the British government had always insisted that the Americans do their trading with England, shipping tobacco, furs, fish, and much else to England so that British merchants could make a profit on them, and the British government could put duties on them. The Americans, naturally, wanted to ship their goods to whatever country would give them the best deal. Among the most important markets for American goods were the islands of the West Indies, where American merchants could profitably trade foodstuffs for slaves and sugar. Sugar was especially important to New Englanders, for molasses was made from sugar, and rum was made from molasses. Rum was a major item of export from New England.

Trading with the West Indies would have been acceptable if the Americans had done business with only the British islands there. However, they also traded with Spanish and French colonies where molasses could be bought cheaper. Trade with the French, with whom the English had been at war for decades, was particularly obnoxious. There were laws against it, and so far as England was concerned, this trade was simply smuggling. Nevertheless it went on, and there was no secret about it. In 1760, a man named George Spencer tried to get a New York newspaper to publish his exposé of the illegal trade with the enemy. The paper refused to publish it, a mob pelted him with garbage and manure, and he landed in jail, although eventually the British got him out.

The story makes clear how far British and American attitudes had drifted apart. It seemed obvious to poor George Spencer, and his British supporters, that doing business with the loathed French was not merely illegal, but unpatriotic, indeed shameful. The Americans saw it differently. In their view British laws against trading with the French were an interference with their rights—as well as their ability to turn a profit—and they took it as almost a patriotic duty to pelt Spencer with rotten fruit.

Nonetheless, in 1760 the English authorized the Writs of Assistance, open-ended search warrants different from the customary ones that specified the time, place, and items to be searched. Some Boston merchants objected to this supposed violation of traditional "rights" and decided to fight the Writs of Assistance in court. As one of their lawyers, they hired a spirited speaker named James Otis. Other lawyers made reasoned pleas, based on points of law. Otis, however, made a fiery speech, one so stirring that John Adams said it was one of the most remarkable ones he ever heard. "Then and there the child Independence was born," Adams claimed.

Otis emphasized the idea of natural rights. The idea that human beings had certain natural rights was an old one. It was also a radical one, for under it people could claim that they had a right to almost anything. The people could give up some of their rights, if they chose, through their elected representatives in a legislature; but they were not bound to obey laws imposed on them by outsiders. Actually, Otis lost the case in court; but it was clear that the Writs of Assistance laws could not be enforced in America, and they were never really put to use.

The theory that Americans were not bound by the rules and regulations coming out of London was, by the early 1760s, much talked about by lawyers, politicians, and philosophers. It appears, however, that the British government, and the British people in general, did not realize how strongly Americans were coming to resent British rule over them. If they had, Parliament might have been more cautious in what it did next.

England had piled up huge debts in fighting its series of wars with France, and a good deal of money had gone toward driving the French out of North America and off the backs of the Americans. The national debt had grown to well over 145 million pounds, a huge sum for the time. (An English workingman might earn two pounds a year.) Few people in England expected the Americans to pay for the wars with the French, even though the most recent of those wars was fought largely for colonial interests. Taxes in England had to be raised to pay off this debt, so it seemed reasonable for the Americans to pay the salaries of imperial officials and the British troops stationed in America for the protection of Americans. Even many Americans agreed that this was just. In order to raise this money, the English government decided to make a real effort at collecting duties in American ports. It reduced the tax on each gallon of molasses brought into the colonies, but strengthened the ability of customs officials to collect it. The law laying this tax is called the Sugar Act. Most historians today think that this was by no means an unreasonable tax—one which Americans could well enough pay, especially as the money was to be used for their own protection.

But many American merchants objected, and they liked to state the question not as to whether they could afford the tax but rather as a constitutional issue, a matter of principle. Once again it was James Otis who pushed the matter to an extreme. A committee he headed reported that

Benjamin Franklin, one of America's greatest statesmen, was among the first to insist that Americans had to "join, or die," as his cartoon declares. This portrait by Charles Willson Peale shows him in his well-known spectacles.

measures like the Sugar Act "have a tendency to deprive the colonies of some of their most essential rights as British subjects . . . particularly the right of assessing their own taxes." In other words, no taxation without representation.

Next, in 1765, the British government decided to establish a "stamp" tax in America. Stamp taxes had been levied in England for some time. What it meant was that many types of legal documents, newspapers, and other papers had to include a special stamp provided by the government at an extra cost, which amounted to a tax. Once again, historians have concluded that the Stamp Tax would not have been a heavy financial burden on Americans. But by now, the mood in the colonies was belligerent.

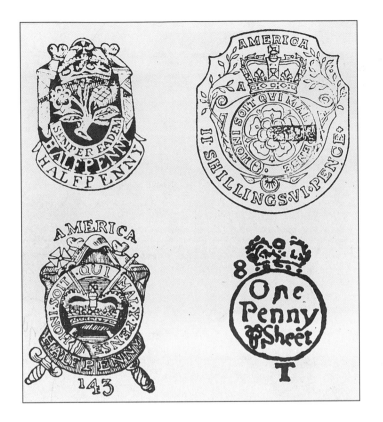

Various stamps the British applied to goods sold in America.

Americans believed that the British were trying to push them around, and they were determined to resist. Lines were being drawn in the sand, and a sense of crisis was in the air.

One of the first to bring matters to a head was Patrick Henry of Virginia. Henry was one of the leaders of the "radicals" in Virginia, determined to stir up trouble. He was young and had a powerful presence. His eyes were deep-set and piercing, his eyebrows thick, his cheeks hollow. He rarely smiled. He was, basically, an angry man. A few years earlier, while arguing a case in court, Henry had expounded Otis's natural rights theory and attacked the law in question, declaring that George III "from being the father of his people degenerated into a tyrant, and forfeits all rights to his subjects' obedience." Henry now, in response to the Stamp Act, laid some resolutions before the Virginia legislature saying that taxes levied from Britain without American consent would "destroy American freedom." He went even further, and said that anyone who supported these British taxes was "an enemy to his majesty's colony"—that is, Virginia. The Virginia legislature

One of America's greatest orators was Patrick Henry, who could hold an audience for hours with his cries for freedom.

was not prepared to go as far as Patrick Henry was, and cut out some of his inflammatory remarks before passing the resolutions. But they were widely printed around America as Henry had originally proposed them, and this further inflamed Americans and hardened their determination to withstand British controls.

Americans decided to fight the Stamp Act. In towns and villages from the Carolinas to New Hampshire they formed themselves into bands that they called "Sons of Liberty," and insisted that they were willing to fight the Stamp Act to the death.

In Massachusetts, the Assembly sent out a call to the other legislatures asking for a meeting of representatives from all colonies to decide what to do about the stamp taxes. When Parliament learned about the proposed meeting it grew angry, but for the moment did nothing.

The Americans, however, were not waiting. On the night of August 14, a Boston group, presumably Sons of Liberty, put together an effigy—that is, a life-sized dummy—of Andrew Oliver, who had been appointed as distributor of the hated stamps, and hung it from a tree. The next day the

Another ardent fighter for American independence was John Adams of Massachusetts. He fought the Stamp Act, represented America in France during the Revolution, and became the second president.

governor ordered his sheriff to take it down, but the sheriff refused, saying that his deputies would be at risk of their lives if they tried to do it. The governor's council also refused to do anything. All afternoon a crowd gathered, and when evening came they marched to a new building Oliver was putting up, and tore it down. They then marched to Oliver's house, beheaded the effigy, and broke some windows. Next they went to nearby Fort Hill, where they burned the effigy in a bonfire. They then went back to Oliver's house and broke in, looking for poor Oliver, who had long since fled.

News of the mob action by the Sons of Liberty swept through the colonies and others quickly followed the Massachusetts example. In Newport, Rhode Island, a mob made up three effigies of men who supported the Stamp Act. The men fled to a British ship that was in Newport harbor. That day came news of a second riot in Boston, during which the house of Governor Hutchinson was broken into and seriously damaged. Emboldened, the Newport mob came together again, and tore into the houses of the three men who had dared to stand up for the Stamp Act. In one house they sliced up valuable paintings, smashed fragile scientific instruments, heaved a sizable library of books down a well, and stole what they wanted. The stamp agent in Newport was forced to resign.

As news of the Newport and Boston riots spread, other Stamp distributors took the hint, and resigned. One who did not resign was Zachariah Hood of Maryland. A mob came to his house and pulled it down. Hood still refused to resign his office, and the mob forced him to flee for his life. He eventually landed in New York, where a mob of New Yorkers in support of the Marylanders found him and finally forced him to resign. And so it went through the colonies. In Connecticut, Jared Ingersoll, like Hood, tried to stand firm. A mob marched him from New Haven to Hartford, threatening to lynch him on the way if he did not resign. Prudently, he quit the job.

Then in October, leaders from the colonies met in New York to work out a unified stand against Parliament. A few of the delegates to this Stamp Act Congress, as it is called, were radicals. But the majority were more moderate men, like John Dickinson of Delaware and Pennsylvania, looking for a peaceable way out of the tussle with England. Even James Otis, serving as a delegate from Massachusetts, retreated from his natural-rights views. Thus, in resolutions written by Dickinson, the Congress allowed that it esteemed "our connection with and dependence on Great Britain, as one of our greatest blessings." But with greater emphasis it insisted that Americans had, if not natural rights, at least all the rights and privileges of Englishmen—especially the right to levy their own taxes. November 1, 1765, the day the Stamp Act was to go into effect, was observed throughout the colonies as a day of mourning, with church bells slowly tolling and effigies hung and burned in public places.

It was not all mob action. Very quickly merchants throughout the colonies agreed to establish a boycott on British goods, insisting that they would do without them until the Stamp Act was repealed. The boycott was not complete, but it was nonetheless very effective.

The British Parliament was now in a quandary. On one hand, it was clear that the Stamp Act could not be enforced. On the other hand, the Parliament could not simply give in to mobs and rioters, or it might as well stop trying to govern the rebellious colonies altogether.

They had yet another problem. Officially, ships could not leave American ports without permission written on the loathed stamped paper. American shippers, shipowners, and ship captains were leery of setting sail without this official permission: the British might not be able to enforce their laws on American soil, but with their mighty fleet they could do so on the seas, and the Americans might well have their ships and cargoes confiscated. With embargoes, stamps, and riots, trade with England suddenly came to a halt.

This halt to trading was hard on many colonists, but they were prepared to bear the burden in order to get their rights. It was even harder on British merchants, who were in a sense innocent bystanders. Not only were they cut off from lucrative business; they were also unable to collect the substantial amounts of money American importers owed them, simply because the Americans were not going to pay until the dispute was settled. Merchants in English cities like London, Liverpool, and Manchester began to put heavy pressure on Parliament to end the fight. One merchant reported, "The present situation of the colonies alarms every person who has any connection with them . . . the avenues of trade are all shut up. . . . We have no remittances [payments], and are at our wits' end for want of money to fulfill our engagement with tradesmen."

It was not only the merchants who were hurt: ordinary workers making things that were sold to the colonies, like cloth and clothing, glass, and tools, were finding themselves out of work. English workers were getting restless, and the government was afraid that they, like the Americans, might also riot, though for different reasons.

The British government was in a dilemma, and kept dancing from one foot to the next; indeed, there were three different prime ministers in

1766 alone. An example of such a dance was given by the famous British statesman, William Pitt, in a speech calling for a repeal of the Stamp Act. Pitt began by saying that the Parliament did *not* have the right to tax the colonists. But he added that the British Parliament "had, hath, and of right ought to have, full power and authority to make laws and statutes of sufficient force and validity to bind the colonies and people of America, subjects of the crown of Great Britain, in all cases whatsoever." Pitt was trying to have it both ways, and in the end that was the course that Parliament itself took. It repealed the Stamp Act, but at the same time, it issued a Declaratory Act which insisted that Parliament nonetheless had the right to tax the colonists if it wanted to.

Here was the hard nut that neither side could crack. In fact, the Stamp Tax was financially meaningless—it would have amounted to about a shilling a year per American at a time when a normal wage was two or three shillings a day. It was not the money; it was the principle of the thing. And so it was with the British: they were willing to drop the tax, so long as it was understood that they had the *right* to impose it. In any case, tempers cooled and trade between England and the colonies revived.

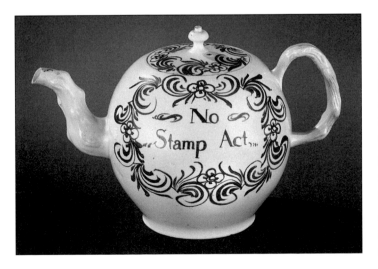

This teapot was actually made in England for sale in the American colonies during the uproar over the Stamp Act, a good indication that many English people sided with the Americans. Teapots were widely popular in America.

CHAPTER III

Taxes and Tea

B
ut nothing was really settled. The Stamp Act was repealed, but as one historian puts it, ". . . the candles that burned in celebration of repeal had scarcely stopped smoking when the colonists found themselves in a new quarrel with the mother country."

This was triggered when the British government, still eager to get money out of the colonists, decided to make the colony governments pay for food and housing for the British troops stationed in America. Once again, it seemed reasonable for the Americans to help support troops that were there for their protection, and many Americans generally accepted that idea, though some questioned why soldiers whose mission was to fight Indians were quartered in coastal cities. They smelled a rat: the new regulation reminded them suspiciously of a sneaky way of taxing them. In most places they responded by either coming up with only a portion of the money or by saying that they were giving the food and lodging as a gift of their own free will. But in New York, Sons of Liberty clashed with bayonet-wielding soldiers, an action that was repeated several years later with injuries on both sides at the Battle of Golden Hill.

This attitude annoyed—indeed angered—a lot of the British, even many in Parliament who had voted to repeal the Stamp Act. The English were aware that, burdened with the large war debt, they were paying much heavier taxes than the Americans were. In May 1767, angry members of Parliament decided to lower taxes at home, and make up the difference by laying duties on a number of things Americans imported in quantity from England, like glass, lead, paper, paints, and tea.

Now it was the Americans' turn to be angry. So far as they were concerned, it was the same old story—taxation without representation. The news of what are now called the Townshend Acts, after the chief financial minister for England whose idea they were, reached America in September 1767. Within days there was a meeting in Boston chaired by the fiery James Otis, to work out a

George III has been much maligned in American history, in part for good reason. His unwillingness to give any ground in the dispute between England and the American colonies led to the Revolution and ultimately the formation of the United States of America. But George III was also a thoughtful husband and father and a loyal friend. He was, at times, certainly insane and a paradoxical human being.

way of fighting off the Townshend taxes. A great many people had disapproved of the riots that had followed the Stamp Act, even though they hated the Act itself. This time it was decided to work by peaceful means. The merchants would revive the boycott of a wide range of British goods, including clothes, jewelry, coaches, watches, and other things.

This meeting was widely reported in newspapers around the colonies and the papers remained full of the story for months. Very important in working up public opinion was a series of articles written by John Dickinson called "Letters from a Farmer in Pennsylvania to the Inhabitants of the British Colonies." Dickinson said that the new taxes on Americans would "sink them into slaves." When a man like Dickinson with a reputation for reason and moderation used such strong terms, it was clear that the American resistance to the Townshend taxes was going to be extremely firm.

In order to make this resistance sure, in February 1768, the Massachusetts Legislature issued the famous "Circular Letter," drawn up by Samuel Adams, which was sent off to the legislatures of all the other colonies. The letter was basically a restatement of the old principle of

As implacable in his own way as the king of England, Massachusetts patriot Samuel Adams, one of the strongest fighters for American freedom, believed early in the game that the colonies had to become independent.

no taxation without representation. It argued that a person had "an essential, unalterable right" to keep what he had; it could be taken away from him only with his consent—which in this case meant through his representatives in a legislature. Very quickly the legislatures of New Hampshire, Virginia, Maryland, Connecticut, Rhode Island, Georgia, and South Carolina came out in support of the Massachusetts Circular Letter.

By this time officials in America, especially the customs officers who were supposed to collect the Townshend duties, had discovered that they could not do so. In recent months they had seized six ships for carrying illegal cargo. Americans had simply taken three of these ships back by force, and two more were given back by American courts that refused to convict American "smugglers." Then, in June, a British warship sailed into Boston Harbor and seized a ship belonging to the wealthy Boston merchant John Hancock. Three days later a mob attacked the "guilty" Boston customs officials, who fled to the safety of the British warship.

The British now believed that law and order was about to break down completely—*their* law and order, in any case. They sent four regiments of British troops to Boston. One hundred Massachusetts towns sent representatives to a meeting to protest the arrival of these "troops of occupation." Some of the more unruly of the Sons of Liberty were ready to fight right then and there, and if they had got their way the American Revolution might have begun in 1768. But cooler heads prevailed.

Now all sorts of rumors flew around Boston, saying that the troops had come to put the city under martial law, thus taking away everybody's freedoms, and to arrest some of the leaders of the American resistance to British rule. But the British troops did none of these things, and for the moment, at least, armed resistance did not break out in Boston.

More important than riots in Boston was the fact that the new boycott of British goods was working. In January 1769, there appeared a letter in a London newspaper, probably written by Benjamin Franklin, who was in London representing Pennsylvania. The letter claimed that the

Townshend taxes had brought in thirty-five hundred pounds, while the boycott had cost British merchants and their workers well over seven million pounds. The letter also said that it would take twenty-five thousand British soldiers ten years and 100 million pounds to subdue a revolution in the colonies. Once again the British government was faced with the old problem: It obviously had to back down from the Townshend taxes, but it had also to assert its right to tax.

In January 1770, Lord Frederick North began a twelve-year reign as prime minister. North was an arrogant man who felt strongly the right of Parliament to dominate events. He looked for a way out of the dilemma. He decided that the Townshend duties would, like the Stamp Act, be repealed, except for the duty on tea, which would remain as a symbol of Parliament's right to tax. That right would be made clear in a preamble to the repeal act. Some in Parliament wanted to drop the duty on tea as well, the better not to stir up the colonists. But Parliament voted to keep the tax on tea.

It is important for us to see that American attitudes toward Britain, and the struggle for what the colonists took to be their rights, kept changing. During the French and Indian War, when the colonies clearly needed the protection of the British army and navy, few Americans were unwilling to accept British authority. In the years after 1763, when the peace treaty with the French was signed, Americans were clear in their minds that Parliament should not tax them, but otherwise accepted the right of England to impose on them many kinds of rules and regulations. By 1770, a few more radical Americans were questioning *any* kind of British authority; over the next few years a great many more would follow.

Later, Massachusetts Governor Thomas Hutchinson, who was of course an appointee of the king, wrote, "At first the supreme authority [of Parliament] seemed to be admitted, the cases of taxes only exempted; but the exceptions gradually extended from one case to another, until it included all cases whatsoever."

(above) This cartoon shows American patriots tarring and feathering an exciseman, or tax collector. He has a noose around his neck, suggesting that he might be hanged. In fact, none of the excisemen were killed, in part because most of them quickly resigned from their jobs.

(right) The threat of hanging was always present for excisemen, however. Many were hanged "in effigy"—that is, a dummy stuffed with straw was hanged, and in some cases publicly beheaded. This is an effigy of Zachariah Hood, tax collector from Maryland.

Or to put it another way, originally the Americans had seen the British as children see their parents—a nuisance, perhaps, and inclined to be bossy, but nonetheless on their side. By 1770, many Americans no longer believed that the British Parliament was on their side. Parliament—though not yet the king—was seen as an adversary; an adversary that could not be permitted complete authority.

People have speculated ever since whether the situation could have been saved. Even at the time, solutions were being offered. One that came up frequently was the idea of electing some of the colonists to the British Parliament. That would have given the Americans the "representation" they needed in order to be taxed. It appears that the British government would have accepted the scheme. The colonists would have none of it. They saw clearly that they would have only a few members in Parliament—according to one plan, about thirty out of the four hundred or five hundred who usually voted. They would be powerless to protest American interests. Representation would be token, and therefore worthless.

Another idea, which historians have discussed, was for the creation of some kind of "federal" system, much like what eventually happened in Canada. In such a plan an American parliament would have been free to run local affairs as they saw fit, while the English government would manage foreign affairs for the general good of everybody. Such a solution would have been acceptable to most Americans before about 1776, and would have kept America inside the British Empire. As sensible as it sounds today, it was too radical for those times, for to the British Parliament it would have seemed like independence for the colonies.

If there was, by 1770, any hope for reconciliation between English and Americans, it disappeared in New England certainly, and probably in several other colonies, on March 5 of that year. The British troops stationed in Boston took part-time jobs and girlfriends from local men and were thoroughly hated by the local citizens. From time to time little mobs would harass the soldiers, cursing them or even throwing things at them.

This caricature shows poor Britain suffering as its limbs, labeled Virginia, Pennsylvania, New York, and New England, are lopped off. It was designed by Benjamin Franklin in 1774 as a warning to England that it stood in danger of losing its valuable American colonies.

On March 5, a crowd began to abuse a sentry in front of the Custom House, throwing garbage and snowballs at him. A guard of seven soldiers and a captain was sent out to rescue him. The guard pushed through the crowd and collected the sentry. But when the British soldiers turned around to take the sentry away, it seemed clear that the crowd would not let them pass. Some of the soldiers fired. Three Americans were killed instantly and two others mortally wounded.

People in Boston and surrounding towns were outraged, and began to prepare themselves to battle the British troops. Once again the leaders of the angry citizens, fearful of the blood that might be spilled, managed to calm things down. But they also demanded that British troops be withdrawn from the city and stationed in Fort William, on an island in Boston

Harbor. Governor Hutchinson saw that he had to accept this demand. When the British left Boston the citizens considered that they had won a great victory. Years later, John Adams—who made a habit of declaring American Independence—said, "On that night the foundations of American independence were laid."

Yet despite what came to be known as the Boston Massacre, things returned to normal for a time. With the repeal of the Townshend duties,

This is Paul Revere's famous engraving of the Boston Massacre, showing British troops firing into the jeering crowd.

the boycott of British goods slowly dropped away, although not without a good deal of protest from some who thought it ought to continue as long as there was still even a token duty on tea. But most merchants decided they needed the business more than the principle, and gradually trade with England started up again—even tea was imported and the despised duty on it was paid.

Yet the British continued to search for ways to assert their authority over the unruly colonists. They decided that the British government, not the Massachusetts Assembly, would pay the salary of Governor Hutchinson and the royal judges. It might seem that the people of Massachusetts would be pleased by no longer having to pay these salaries, but

The afternoon tea ceremony was an important social event for many Americans. People who could afford it had elaborate silver and china tea services. In this reenactment, two colonial dames are having a good gossip over their tea.

they were not, for so long as they could withhold the salaries of officials they had some control over them. Now even this club was gone.

In November 1772, Bostonians created what was called a Committee of Correspondence. This committee drew up a list of grievances to send to all Massachusetts towns asking them their views and urging them to set up similar committees. Other colonies followed the Massachusetts example. Virginia's committee, for example, included Patrick Henry and Thomas Jefferson.

Still, trouble might have been avoided. However, for reasons having little to do with the colonies, the British decided to let their East India Company sell tea directly from the East Indies to America—and at a lower price than it could be bought elsewhere. For all practical purposes, this created a monopoly for the company on this popular, even essential, herb. This system would have the effect of forcing Americans to pay the hated tea duty.

American blood was now up, and along the seaboard committees were formed to prevent ships from landing their cargoes of tea. In New York, Philadelphia, and other port cities leaders organized opposition and threatened bodily harm. Ship captains, faced with such unpleasant welcoming committees, agreed to turn around and take their tea back to England or somewhere else to sell. But in Boston tough-minded Governor Hutchinson decided to force a showdown.

The citizenry, Bostonians and others from neighboring towns, were ready to fight. When three ships carrying tea as well as other cargo arrived in Boston Harbor, they were boarded by patriots who took control of them. Eventually the ships were brought up to a dock, and there they stood for days while everybody involved tried to maneuver for advantage, some trying to land the tea, some trying to send it home, some looking for compromise.

But no compromise was coming. On Thursday, December 16, 1773, some five thousand people crowded into Old South Church. A cold rain was falling. All day they debated and listened to speeches. When it was clear that the tea ships would not be sent home, a signal was given. The people swept out of the church, and down to the docks. Some small, well-organized groups, including men loosely disguised as Indians, boarded the ships, probably no more than sixty people altogether. While a huge crowd on shore stood and watched in silence, they hoisted the wooden chests of tea up onto a dock, split the chests open with hatchets, and dumped the tea into the harbor. The tide was out, the water low, and the tea piled up in great heaps, which had to be pushed aside so more could be dumped out. Within three hours the whole cargo of tea from the three ships, worth around nine hundred thousand pounds ($1.5 million to $2 million today) was dumped into the sea. It had been, indeed, a mammoth tea party.

An engraving of the Boston Tea Party. The members of the party worked swiftly and quietly, hoisting great chests of tea onto deck, splitting the chests open with axes, and dumping the tea into the water. The tide was out, and the tea rose so high that it had to be shoved aside to make room for more.

CHAPTER IV

Lexington, Concord, and Bunker Hill

The response of the British government to the Boston Tea Party was to crack down. Not all British leaders agreed. Some, like William Pitt and the famous conservative Edmund Burke, argued for leniency. America's real value to England, they pointed out, was in the profits made from trade. Revenue from taxes and political control for its own sake were not worth the expenditure of time, money, and goodwill. They believed also that it was unjust for the British to exert great control over the American colonies and further attempts to do so would drive the Americans to rebellion.

But George III, his chief minister Lord North, and at least three-quarters of Parliament wanted to see the colonists brought sharply to heel. The government now passed what have been called the Coercive Acts. They were aimed principally at Massachusetts, which the British government correctly saw—along with Patrick Henry's Virginia—as the hotbed of revolutionary spirit. The idea was to punish Massachusetts for the destruction of the tea. Many Massachusetts officials were now to be appointed by the British government, instead of chosen by the colonists. Meetings of colonists—even traditional town meetings—could not be held without approval of the governor—Boston Harbor was to be shut up and the trade choked off.

The Massachusetts House of Representatives now urged a renewal of non-importation. But patriots in Providence, New York, and Philadelphia called instead for a general meeting of the colonies, and in September 1774, a group of men met in Philadelphia to debate the fate of America. There were among them some conservatives who were looking for a way to make peace with the British government. But the majority were strongly of the opinion that Parliament should not, could not, and must not have complete control over the colonists, who ought to be free to lay their own taxes and run their own local affairs. The delegates to this First Continental Congress agreed that somebody had to be in charge of international trade and defense of the British Empire, and allowed that Parliament should have control over foreign affairs. But otherwise the Americans had to be free to govern themselves.

The colonists were toying with the dangerous idea of "the principle of human equality." This idea is so basic to the American spirit that we may find it hard to believe that it has not always been accepted. Indeed, only a few years earlier Lord North, the British government's chief minister, had said, "I can never acquiesce in the absurd opinion that all men are equal." He meant equal in political rights, of course. But by now the American leaders had concluded that they were, in fact, equal, in which case there was no reason to accept the authority over them of men not of their choosing.

The British government, still trying to find its way out of the morass it had sunk itself into, now offered the colonists a scheme that had come up before: they could tax themselves and send the money to England. But by this time this did not seem like much of a concession to the Americans, and they turned it down.

Now, though many Americans believed that they would have to fight, more thought that if they rallied their militias, the British would back

This cartoon shows the Tory editor of a newspaper trying to persuade some American sailors not to fight against England, saying "You will get hard knocks on the pate [the head]! You will spend your years in English prisons." The second sailor replies, "Why tis all my eye Jack. Shiver my limbs but this fellow is an English dishclout."

down. New Englanders assumed that the confrontation would take place in Massachusetts, which had been at the forefront of resistance to the British. Here men began to prepare. We should keep it in mind that every colony in America had an organized militia—companies of soldiers who met a few times a year to stay prepared to fight whatever enemies attacked them. In the past the enemies had been the French and the Indians. That threat died in 1763 with the end of the French and Indian War, and the militias had become lax in their training. But now they had a new enemy to worry about—the British army—and the Massachusetts militias began to prepare themselves in earnest. Among other things, they collected gunpowder and other military supplies in the village of Concord.

The British knew about the military supplies at Concord. Through the early-winter months of 1775, they occasionally made training marches out of Boston into the countryside. The local people grew tenser, and more fearful. What were the British up to? Did they intend to capture, and perhaps hang, the resistance leaders, like John Hancock and Samuel Adams? Nobody knew, and as the winter ebbed and spring came, the nerves of Massachusetts patriots were wound up tight.

But the Americans were not just worrying. They were getting themselves well organized, through committees of one kind and another. They organized companies of "minutemen," who would come on the run if the British attacked anywhere. They set about discovering what they could about British intentions. By early April it was clear that something was up—probably, the Americans believed, the British would march on Concord to capture the munitions stored there, and perhaps also capture the colonial leaders. In Boston a silversmith named Paul Revere, who also doubled as a dispatch rider when urgent messages had to be carried from Boston to other cities, was assigned the job of warning the leaders in Concord if the British marched. On the evening of April 18, the British did indeed march in silence out of Boston. Word reached Revere and another dispatch rider, named William Dawes. They instantly set off from Boston by different routes, heading for Concord. As Revere went he contacted designated local political and military leaders in villages along a prearranged route. These men in turn sent out other riders to towns to the north and west.

At midnight Revere reached Lexington, where Hancock and Adams were hiding out. He arrived with a clatter at the place where they were staying, and was told not to make so much noise because everybody was sleeping. "Noise," Revere replied, according to legend. "You'll have noise enough before long. The regulars are coming." He waited there until Dawes, coming by a longer route, rode up, and they set off for Concord, along with Dr. Samuel Prescott, who was returning to Concord after a late evening visit with his girlfriend. About halfway there they were jumped by some British officers. Dawes fled, Revere was captured, and despite the famous legend, the warning was carried to Concord by Prescott.

Meanwhile, in Lexington as the first faint light of day was rising in the east, seventy minutemen gathered on the green in the center of town. The British force of more than six hundred would have to pass the green on the way to Concord. The commander of the minutemen, Captain John Parker, probably should have realized that his small force had no chance against the British, and retreated. But he did not. The British hove into sight and swung around to face the minutemen. The British officer, Major John Pitcairn, shouted to Parker, "Lay down your arms, you damned rebels, and disperse."

Parker at last saw there was no point in fighting, and ordered his men to disband. They did not give up their guns, however. Pitcairn shouted again, "Lay down your arms." But the Americans continued to drift away, holding their guns. There was a shot—the shot heard 'round the world, it was later said. Who fired it is not known. Major Pitcairn later insisted that it had been an American; he had given no order to fire. The most plausible explanation put forth is that there were several nearly simultaneous shots, one probably from an American spectator and another from a British officer on horseback. Perhaps a British musket fired as a soldier answered the order to present arms. We will never know who or which side fired the shot heard 'round the world. The first shot or shots were immediately followed by a volley. Pitcairn shouted to his men to cease firing, but they did not. The Americans began to run. When the firing was over eight Americans were dead and ten wounded. Only one British soldier was hurt. It was a battle of little military significance, but the American Revolution had begun.

The British marched to Concord. The Americans managed to hide most of their munitions, but the British captured some. Then, as they

This steel engraving by Alonzo Chappel shows the Americans firing on British troops as they retreat from Concord. The artist created the picture from his imagination, but the general idea is probably correct.

turned around to march back to Boston, American minutemen, now joined by organized militia companies, were pouring in from the countryside all around, hundreds of them. "It seems as if men came down from the clouds," somebody said later. All along the road back to Boston, armed Americans sometimes drawn up in regimental formations, but more often dispersed in small units in the woods and behind stone walls, fired at the British as they marched in formation. European armies had always fought in formation, two armies drawn up in order facing each

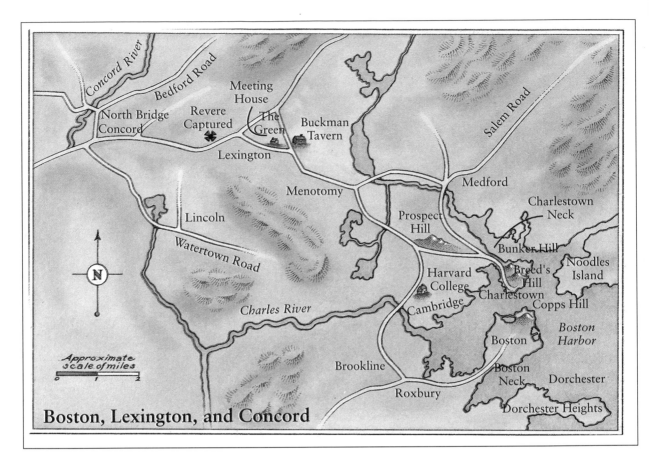

Boston, Lexington, and Concord

other. This rain of bullets from behind walls and around the corner of barns bewildered the British soldiers. They fell steadily. The American force increased as men continued to rain down "from the skies." The British began to run out of ammunition. In terror, they began to run.

The British relief troops, requested hours earlier, finally arrived from Boston, and for the moment the Americans backed off a bit. But militiamen continued to arrive—134 from Watertown, 59 from Medford, 337 from Dedham, and more from elsewhere until there were two thousand Americans ready to resume the attack. They continued to pour fire into British ranks from their hiding places and on several occasions from formations directly facing the British in European style. Finally, at evening, the British reached Boston and safety. The battle was over.

In fact, only seventy-three British were killed, one hundred seventy-four wounded, and twenty-six missing. The Americans had forty-nine dead, forty-one wounded. But the fight had finally convinced at least some of the English that the Americans not only could, but would, fight. One officer said, ". . . nor will the insurrection here turn out so despicable as it is perhaps imagined at home. For my part, I never believed, I confess, that they would have attacked the King's troops, or have had the perseverance I found in them yesterday."

About three weeks later a Second Continental Congress gathered in Philadelphia to make plans for the war. A few men among them still hoped that war could be prevented, and they got up a petition to George III suggesting that if the colonial legislatures could be seen as equal to Parliament, they would stay loyal to the king. This so-called "Olive Branch Petition" was rejected: George III insisted that Parliament must be the paramount authority in the British Empire. And that was the end of the peace effort.

Another thing the Second Continental Congress did was to appoint an experienced soldier from Virginia as head of what would be the American Army. He was George Washington, who had fought with the British against the French in the French and Indian War. (For Washington's exploits in that conflict, see *The French and Indian War*, the fourth book of this series.) But before Washington could get to Boston to assume command, fighting broke out again.

In mid-June the Americans got word that the British intended to fortify the high ground on a point of land that overlooked Boston. The Americans decided they had better take it over first, and on the evening of June 16, a small detachment of not more than three hundred men marched into the area, intending to build a fortification on Bunker Hill. They decided, however, to construct the fort on nearby Breed's Hill. All night the men sweated, and swore to throw up a dirt wall six feet high.

When the British awoke in the morning and saw the little fort on

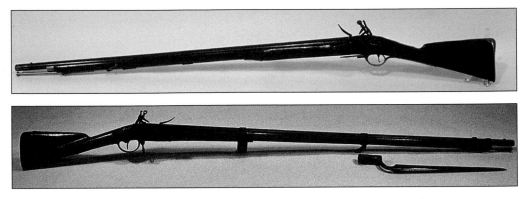

(top) One of the most famous weapons in the Revolution was the Brown Bess musket. It was standard equipment in the British army, and thousands were issued to the American militia before the split with England. As a consequence they were widely used by Americans, too.
(bottom) After the Battle of Saratoga, when it appeared that the Americans had a chance to win, French support increased dramatically. The French supplied thousands of these Charleville muskets. One is shown here with its bayonet unfixed.

Breed's Hill they quickly began to bombard it from cannon on ships in the harbor. The bombardment had little effect, and it was clear that the British would have to attack. The British decided to land men on the shore below the hill, out of range from the fort. This force would then march along the beach around the base of the hill and attack the fort from the rear. However, before they could get organized, the Americans built a breastwork down the slope of the hill toward the water until it reached a fence there. This was farmland; there were stone walls everywhere, and the Americans used the stones to make a sturdy defensive line down to the water's edge.

Then they waited. At one o'clock the British troops landed. General Howe told his men that he would not ask them "to go a step further than I would go myself as your head." He would lead the troops himself. From the ships came a steady bombardment of the American position. Howe sent one group of men against the redoubt at the top of the hill to keep their attention, and sent another force against the breastwork running down to the water, hoping to break through and outflank the redoubt.

As news of the British attack spread through Boston, people began to gather along the river shore, sitting on rooftops, up on hills. As if at a baseball game, they watched the redcoats roll steadily on toward the hastily erected breastwork along the shore. The sweating redcoats, each weighted down with a hundred pounds of clothes, equipment, and food, struggled steadily forward over stone walls, through hayfields. As the story goes, the Americans were told to withhold their fire "until you see the whites of their eyes." They waited. On came the British. Then, when they were only a hundred and fifty feet away, they fired. The British line was shattered, and collapsed. Yet again they came. Once more the Americans fired, and the British line wavered and fell back. Yet again they tried; the Americans fired again, and this time the British turned and ran.

The British could not turn the American flank—that is, make an end run and fire at the side rather than the front of the American line. Now they must attack the redoubt directly. They did so, marching up the hill under the full weight of equipment. Once again the Americans fired. In the first blast all twelve officers of Howe's staff were either killed or wounded.

Yet the British would not give up. Again and again they attacked; again and again the Americans scythed them down like so much hay. Finally, however, American gunpowder began to run out. The Americans could not go on. The British swarmed over the redoubt, bayonets flashing. The Americans, without bayonets, fought them, swinging their muskets like clubs. But there was little hope, and the Americans pulled back, fighting as they went. In retreat they suffered more losses than they had taken all afternoon on top of Breed's Hill. But they had shown the British that they could stand up and fight—and win, too, if they had had enough ammunition.

CHAPTER V

The Declaration of Independence

What the Americans took to be glorious victories at Lexington and Concord and Bunker Hill gave them a far too optimistic view of their ability to beat the mighty British army. Two weeks after the battle at Bunker Hill, on July 3, 1775, George Washington arrived, appointed by the Continental Congress to command the troops around Boston. His job was to put together an army out of the disorderly groups of minutemen, organized militias, and miscellaneous individual new volunteers from all over New England—to the number of about 14,500. As soon as he could, he placed some cannon on a high point overlooking Boston. The British realized that they were in a dangerous position, and withdrew from Boston. And now the war began in earnest.

Very quickly Washington learned that what the Americans took to be glorious victories at Bunker Hill and along the road from Concord to Boston had given them a much too high opinion of their ability to beat the mighty British army. The American Revolution would drag on for years, with the Americans losing more battles than they won. It did not follow a very orderly course.

The British strategy was based on their belief that the rebellion was led by a few rabble-rousers in New England, and if that region could be closed off and controlled, the rest of the colonies would give up their opposition to British arms. British officers were soon to learn that independence sentiment was strong in every colony. Within eighteen months, they abandoned their initial plan to split off New England from the other colonies by taking command of the Hudson River Valley. Instead they sought to take the major cities and dominate the coastland from Maine to Georgia. Ultimately they failed to do this, though they occupied New York City for the whole period 1776 to 1783, and on occasion captured Philadelphia, Charleston, and other port cities. Most often, however, local tactical concerns determined the action. Usually there was no real "front," across which the two armies faced each other. Instead, they fought first here and then there, wherever one general thought he might inflict some damage on the enemy, or gain control of some strategic point—a city, a river junction, a high point.

Each side had its own particular problems to deal with. The British were fighting three thousand miles from home, which meant that bringing in more troops and supplies was difficult to do, and took a long time. Too, as the war went on, American ships became more and more skilled at attacking British ships on the sea, even as they were coming out of the English Channel.

George Washington had plenty of problems of his own. Congress was always short of money and frequently did not send him the things he needed for the war. Often the states did not send what they were supposed to, even when Congress had approved it. Ordinary Americans were both independent-minded and sometimes discouraged by the progress of the war: most soldiers would sign up only for a year at a time, and Washington too often had to depend upon poorly trained and frequently undisciplined militia, who too often went home to tend their farms just when Washington needed them most.

George Washington in a classic pose: on a white horse reviewing troops.

On top of everything, Americans were by no means united in their feelings about the Revolution. Significant numbers felt that independence would be a mistake, and wanted no part of it. John Adams estimated that in 1776 as many as a third of Americans were Loyalists, or Tories, as they were usually called, though modern historians think twenty percent might be a closer guess. In New England they were a minority; in Georgia and South Carolina they were a majority; in the other colonies they may have amounted to about half of the population—a very large number of people in any case. Many of them were rich merchants and landowners; others were professionals, like lawyers, doctors, and Anglican ministers.

But many ordinary farmers and workers joined the British side, too; Loyalists reflected a cross section of American society.

These people did not necessarily believe that Americans should do whatever the English told them to do. Many of them were against the Coercive Acts and other British regulations, and were quite willing to dispute the British on these points. But they did not wish to leave the British Empire, which they thought had value for America. And, of course, they believed that from a military standpoint, the Patriot cause was doomed.

As the war went on, positions on both sides hardened. More and more Loyalists were harassed by Patriots—beaten, tarred, and feathered, perhaps their houses and property taken from them when they fled, in some cases jailed. In the South, warfare between Tories and Patriots was often fierce, with open gun battles occurring frequently. It has been estimated that over two hundred thousand American Loyalists were exiled, or left America for other parts of the British Empire, especially Canada. Thousands joined the British army and died in the same numbers and agony as the Patriots. Nonetheless, Patriot treatment of Loyalists was far more humane than might be expected in a situation where feelings were strong; we can imagine how a Patriot woman who had lost her husband or a son to the British would feel toward her Tory neighbors. Yet America never saw anything like the bloodbath that took place during the French Revolution a decade later. After the war many Loyalists who remained in their hometowns were accepted as before. In addition, the British government compensated some Loyalists who had had their property seized.

There were two other groups in America whose feeling toward the Revolution was decidedly mixed—the Indians and the blacks. When the fighting started, Congress quickly realized that they had better make peace with the Indians, so as not to have to fight them as well as the British. They tried to stop settlers from pushing out onto Indian land. In some places the Indians joined the Continental forces; but generally they sided with the British, for they expected the British to win, and saw in the

The British encouraged the Indians to fight against the Americans, and the Indians tended to do so, assuming that the British would win. This English engraving is an attack on the British use of Indians in the war, which the artist considered inhumane. The fat British official is saying, "Bring me the Scalps and the King our master will reward you." The sign on the Indian's musket says, "Reward for Sixteen Scalps."

war an opportunity to serve their own interests. In the bargain, they might be able to drive the Americans from some of their territory. The Indians thus tended to fight on the British side; but it was not their war, and when they saw things going badly for the British in a battle, they might pull out, as they did during the fighting for Saratoga. As it turned out, choosing to side with the British, while understandable, was a mistake for the Indians, for when peace came the Americans felt that they owed them nothing.

Black slaves, who might be thought to welcome a war against their masters, surprisingly, were also divided about which side to join. The British offered freedom to blacks who served in the army or navy, and thousands of blacks took advantage of these offers. Some American states also offered freedom for serving; and in addition hundreds of free blacks enlisted on the American side. But many felt that their chances for freedom were better with the British, and thousands of them joined the British, or fled with them when they left occupied areas. In the North probably more blacks joined the British rather than the American armies.

Nonetheless, at least five thousand African-Americans served with the Patriot forces. Why would blacks, many of them former slaves, be willing to fight for a nation that was oppressing them? Partly, of course, for those still in slavery, to obtain their freedom. Another reason was that war service was not likely to be much worse than laboring as a slave, and might be more exciting. In other cases they had no choice; masters took them to war with them or sent them as substitutes for drafted sons. Beyond these practical reasons, they were responding to the call for liberty embodied in the Revolution. It seemed to many blacks that a nation to be built on the principle of freedom might share it with them. And in fact, in some northern states a movement to end slavery began to grow.

The South took a different view of it, and many masters insisted that their slaves stay home. But as the war progressed, and manpower grew scarce, the authorities more and more reached out for slaves. Probably the largest number of them did not actually fight, but were used as laborers, driving wagons, building fortifications, hauling supplies. The slaves of Loyalists were considered fair game, and were often confiscated to labor for the army.

Blacks had always worked as seamen on fishing boats and merchant vessels, both as slaves and free, and it was an easy matter for them to switch over to war duty on gunboats. A substantial number of African-Americans served with both the Continental navy and various state navies.

Again, surprisingly, given feelings of the time, most blacks who served were not put in separate units, as they would be in subsequent wars, but were scattered throughout the army, at a time when virtually all white Americans viewed them as inferior in nearly every way. Most blacks fought, and often died, side by side with whites. A famous case was Jordan Freeman. During a British attack on New London, Freeman joined the Patriot forces. They were driven back into Fort Griswold across the Thames from the town. The Americans inflicted heavy casualties on the British, but in the end were forced to surrender. Freeman had been one of the men who had speared a popular British officer. The British bayoneted him to death and then went on to slaughter many of the American captives.

Nonetheless, most blacks were slaves, and slave owners did not wish to risk their property in the war. Far and away the bulk of African-Americans spent the war as they had always lived, laboring in tobacco fields and rice paddies, except when the war closed in on them and they were ordered to build fortifications.

The Tories, the Indians, and the blacks constituted a huge group of people who were either indifferent or actively against the Revolution. But even among the rest of the American population Washington had by no means a unified nation behind him. This was reflected in his continuing difficulties with Congress through the entire war. We must bear it in mind that the colonies did not really think of themselves merely as parts of a large nation. They saw themselves as independent states trying to work together in a common endeavor. New Englanders found Pennsylvania a foreign place, filled with strange people with strange ways. Southerners had always been suspicious of Northerners; and backcountry people did not mix easily with the wealthier, more sophisticated people in coastal towns and cities.

Additionally, each state had its own special interests. A state with enclosed borders, like Maryland, wanted the vaguely defined "western lands" left for the use of the general government; however, some states had long claimed that their lands extended to the Mississippi, and wanted those claims made good. Again, when it was decided to tax each state on the basis of population, the southern states did not want their slaves counted, while the northern ones insisted that they should be. There was constant bickering in Congress.

But the worst problem for Washington—and for the Continental Congress itself—was that it could not order the states to do anything they did not want to. Congress could not demand that the states contribute money for the war, but could only request them to pay up. Washington could not draft men into the army, but again had to depend upon the states to supply them. Washington's major mark of greatness was his political skill at keeping the Congress and the thirteen independent states behind him to the degree that he did.

This was the situation that faced Washington as he watched the British evacuate Boston. He suspected that they would probably now attack New York, which would give them a good port to operate from, and he brought his troops down and established them on Brooklyn Heights, just across the river from Manhattan. On July 2, 1776, the British arrived in New York, unaware that in Philadelphia, not far to the south, the Continental Congress was voting to declare the colonies independent from the British Empire. But it was August before the battle was joined. Washington, still a self-taught commander despite his experience in the French and Indian War, made a serious mistake. He engaged the enemy on the open plains below Brooklyn Heights. We must realize that warfare in those days was often fought by two bodies of men formed up in carefully planned ranks. The soldiers were expected to stand fast no matter how much fire they were taking, and they usually did. Each block of men maneuvered, attacking and counterattacking until one army was destroyed, or broke and ran.

The Americans had been successful on the road out of Concord and at Bunker Hill precisely because they fought from cover, while the British marched and maneuvered in the traditional way. Now Washington allowed himself to be drawn into the European type of war. He was solidly defeated on Long Island, and if General Howe had followed up his victory by pursuing the Americans, the Revolution might have been over almost before it started. But Washington was able to get away with nine thousand men, cannon, and a lot of provisions. He worked his way over to Manhattan, and then north to Harlem Heights, leaving New York to the enemy. The British held New York for the rest of the war, giving them the first-rate port they needed.

The defeat on Long Island taught Washington a major lesson. Henceforward, his strategy would be to avoid open battle with the British unless he was sure he could win. When he reverted to European-style fighting—as at Germantown outside of Philadelphia—he lost. The idea was to run until he had the advantage.

After some inconclusive maneuvering north of New York City, Washington took a position along the Delaware River, in order to protect Philadelphia. Meanwhile, in that city there had occurred one of the most significant events in American history. On July 4, 1776, members of the Continental Congress officially adopted the Declaration of Independence.

This famous document has three parts: a preamble, the main text, which lists the abuses that Americans felt they had suffered at British hands, and a conclusion. It is the preamble that is best known, with its familiar opening lines, "When in the course of human events . . ." and goes on to say: "We hold these truths to be self-evident, that all men are created equal, that they are endowed by their Creator with certain inalienable rights, that among these are Life, Liberty and the Pursuit of Happiness."

The key phrase in this preamble is "endowed by their Creator with certain inalienable rights"—that is, rights that cannot be taken away. Following the opinion of the British philosopher John Locke, the Amer-

Two famous pictures of the Declaration of Independence. The one at left was painted by John Trumbull. The artist traveled around making portraits of the signers and then put them together in this composite painting. Actually, they were not all present at the same time. John Hancock stands at the right. Standing facing him from right are Benjamin Franklin, Thomas Jefferson (who drafted the document), William Livingston, Roger Sherman, and John Adams.

The picture above was adapted from the Trumbull painting by Edward Hicks and is also partly made up.

icans believed that there were "natural," or God-given rights that no king nor Parliament could take away. These people, like Thomas Jefferson who wrote the basic draft of the Declaration of Independence, believed it was obvious that such rights existed; you did not have to prove it. As the Declaration says, they were "self-evident."

Behind this idea was the concept of the "social contract," which had been developed earlier by philosophers like Locke. People in a town, state, or country joined together in a social contract to protect their rights. The first thing they had to do was establish a government for that purpose. These rights, as both English and Americans saw them, included the right to a representative government, a right to trial by jury, the right to assemble and petition the government, the right not to be taxed unless you consented through your representatives in government—in short, your right to life, liberty, and property.

If the government failed to protect the people's rights, or worse, took them away as Americans believed the king and Parliament wanted to do, then the *government* had broken the social contract, and the people had the right and duty to form a new government. In this view, it was the king who was the revolutionary, for he had broken the contract. This was the philosophical position the signers of the Declaration of Independence took.

The Declaration was not, however, solely a philosophical statement. It was intended also to serve certain political purposes. The words were written to shape the opinion of mankind, including, in particular, Americans who had not made up their minds; friends or potential friends in England—even in Parliament; and foreign governments—France in particular—that might provide aid in the contest against England. It was remarkably successful in these efforts.

By 1776, Patriot political leaders were pretending—and some actually believed—that the colonies had never been under Parliament, so they never mention Parliament in the Declaration and concentrate their aim on George III. Previously, Americans, in the main, had professed loyalty to the king, even when they were contesting the rules set up by his government. In the Declaration of Independence they now several times blamed their problems on "the present King of Great Britain." They would no longer be loyal; there was no chance of compromise. Americans would fight to the end.

A cartoon from 1779 showing George III being thrown off his horse, America, although at this point there was no assurance that the horse would be able to throw its master.

CHAPTER VI

The War for American Independence

It was now growing clear to both sides that the end would be long in coming. The British had assumed at the outset that their mighty army, backed by as mighty a fleet which could control the coast where most of America's important towns lay, would be able to sweep aside the impudent rabble who made up America's fighting force. Lexington and Concord, Bunker Hill, and their inability to finish Washington off after the battling in New York, and finally their disastrous defeat at Saratoga in 1777 made the British understand that they were in for a long war.

To the Americans it looked like an even longer and much grimmer prospect. The Continental Army, as it was now called, was poorly trained, lacked bayonets, sufficient arms, and especially shoes and clothing. Desertions were a constant problem, and money an even worse one. And on December 31, 1776, the enlistments of a majority of Washington's troops would be up. The men would go home, leaving Washington with an army of fourteen hundred men, many of them sick.

The military situation was this. General Howe had decided that, with winter coming, he would call off his campaign—the British generally did not fight in America during cold and snowy weather. Howe was comfortably situated in New York, enjoying his social life. He had estab-lished a few strong points from New York down to Philadelphia, among them bases at Trenton and Princeton in New Jersey. Howe's troops, he knew, were spread thin, but it did not seem likely that Washington, situ-ated across the Delaware River, was much of a threat, particularly as he would have to get his troops across the ice-filled river.

Washington's troops were spread even more thinly. He knew that if Howe made any kind of strong attack, he could probably sweep the Continentals aside, and march into Philadelphia, which would give the British control of two of America's most important cities. A defeated American army might simply melt away.

George Washington was by nature a man who liked to attack. During the French and Indian War he had twice made foolhardy stands when he might have done better to hold off, and it had been difficult for him to learn patience. But the war was not going well for the Continentals and to raise American morale and attract foreign aid he must have a victory. Now, he let his basic inclination free. He could not simply sit there and wait for Howe to come after him with his superior forces. Even though the odds were against him, might it not be better to attack? In looking at it cold-bloodedly, it seemed politically and militarily that he had no choice.

The plan he worked out was for three forces of troops to cross the Delaware separately. Washington would lead the main division and all three would join at the British outpost at Trenton. Then they would all join, and if possible attack the posts at Princeton and New Brunswick.

He made the attack early in the morning on the day after Christmas, when the English troops would be sleepy after their holiday celebrations. In fact, the troops were not, in the main, English. Many ordinary English peo-ple felt some sympathy with the Americans in their cry for freedom, and George III had difficulty in raising English troops for the fight. To fill out his army he hired soldiers from various of the small German principalities,

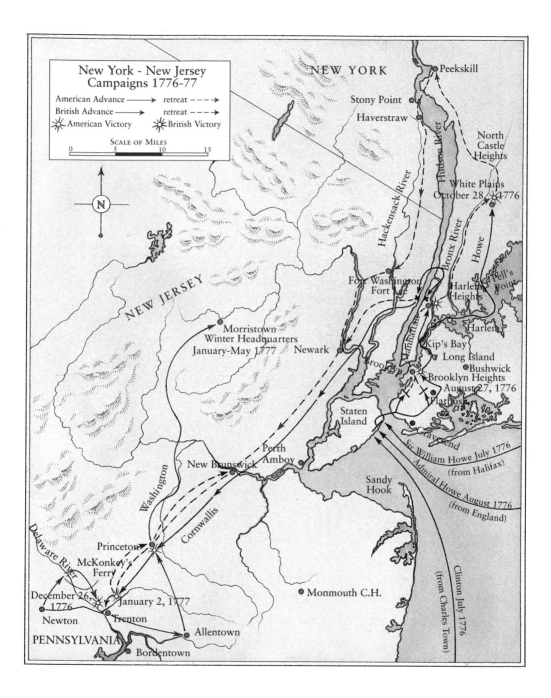

New York - New Jersey
Campaigns 1776-77

American Advance ⟶   retreat ⇢
British Advance ⟶   retreat ⇢
✳ American Victory   ✳ British Victory

SCALE OF MILES

0   5   10   15

N

NEW YORK

Peekskill

Stony Point

Haverstraw

North
Castle
Heights

White Plains
October 28, 1776

Hackensack River

Hudson River

Bronx River

Howe

Fort Washington
Fort Lee

Pell's
Point

Harlem
Heights

Harlem

NEW JERSEY

Morristown
Winter Headquarters
January-May 1777   Newark

Kip's Bay

Long Island

Bushwick

Brooklyn

Brooklyn Heights
August 27, 1776

Flatbush

Staten
Island

Gravesend

Washington

Perth
Amboy

New Brunswick

Sir William Howe July 1776
(from Halifax)

Cornwallis

Sandy
Hook

Admiral Howe August 1776
(from England)

Delaware River

Princeton

McKonkey's
Ferry

December 26,
1776   January 2, 1777

Newton

Trenton

Monmouth C.H.

Clinton July 1776
(from Charles Town)

Allentown

PENNSYLVANIA

Bordentown

especially Hesse; these German troops were generally known as Hessians.

Fortunately for Washington, there was available to him a special kind of boat much used on the Delaware. These boats, called Durham boats after the man who devised them, were poled, although they had sails for use when the wind was strong. They could carry a great deal of freight, and would be more than adequate to move Washington's little armies, and their horses and cannons.

Christmas night, 1776, the men climbed onto the Durham boats. There was a full moon, but the sky was filled with clouds, and the night very dark. The cold was bitter, and chunks of ice racing down the river clunked against the sides of the boats. Few of the men had overcoats. Some of them were actually barefoot, and would be walking on frozen roads.

One of Washington's officers wrote before the embarkation, "It is fearfully cold and raw and a snow-storm is setting in. The wind is northeast and beats in the faces of the men. It will be a terrible night for the soldiers who have no shoes. Some of them tied old rags around their feet, but I have not heard a man complain."

Despite everything, the crossing went smoothly. But it did not go on time. The troops were four hours late getting across and could no longer hope to surprise the enemy at daybreak. Many of the officers, who understood the problem, were downhearted. But not Washington. Said the officer quoted above, "I have never seen Washington so determined as he is now. He stands on the bank of the stream, wrapped in his cloak, superintending the landing of his troops. He is calm and collected, but very determined. The storm is changing to sleet, and cuts like a knife."

So off they marched. After they had gone a little way a message came to Washington from one of his generals saying that the storm was wetting the muskets and they could not fire. Washington replied, "Tell General Sullivan to use the bayonet. I am resolved to take Trenton."

So Washington's twenty-four hundred bedraggled soldiers marched

*One of the most famous of all American historical scenes is Washington cross-
ing the Delaware River with his troops to attack Trenton. Here we see men
poling the boats across while Washington stands, staring out as if he could get
the troops across by sheer will power, which was almost true.*

on. At the outskirts of Trenton the road split. Washington divided his
troops, sending them into town by two routes. Despite everything, they
achieved complete surprise. They burst into town, charging with bayonets, because their muskets were still wet and would not fire. Hessians
fled everywhere before them. The Americans swirled through the wind-
whipped sleet down the streets of Trenton. Some of them ran into houses where they could dry their muskets, and from windows poured fire out
onto the Hessians who were running in disorder from street to street,
looking for safety. There was none.

The Americans brought up some cannons, and began blasting away at
buildings where the Hessians were holed up. The Hessians began to give

up. Singly, in twos and threes, by companies, they threw down their weapons. By nine o'clock in the morning it was over. Washington's ragged band had taken Trenton, almost a thousand prisoners, a thousand muskets, some cannons, even the trumpets and clarinets of the Hessian bands. And a few days later George Washington marched his Hessian prisoners through the streets of Philadelphia. They made a fine contrast with the Americans guarding them—the defeated Hessians in their natty, colorful uniforms, strong and healthy, the victorious Americans in ragged clothes and barefoot. The threat to Philadelphia was now marching through the city's streets, prisoners of war.

Washington's victory at Trenton electrified America. After the loss of New York and the succeeding retreats, Americans had begun to lose confidence in their commander. Now that confidence returned full force. Congress increased his powers, enabling him to carry on the fight.

As a result of the Trenton victory enlistments increased; Washington now had an army of ten thousand men. The dilatory Howe, who preferred to spend his time enjoying himself, was finally aroused. Near the end of August 1777, he arrived at Chesapeake Bay with fifteen thousand troops. Washington battled him at Brandywine Creek, and again at Germantown in a heavy fog. The Americans lost both battles and Howe marched victorious into Philadelphia. Here he once again succumbed to the charms of city social life, and loafed when he should have been marching.

After the losses at Brandywine and Germantown, Washington led his army off to the place that has become an American legend, Valley Forge in Pennsylvania, to lick his wounds. The suffering of the men was immense. Half of them were without shoes, and Washington himself said later, "you might have tracked the army from White Marsh to Valley Forge by the blood of their feet." Many of the men had no trousers or shirts, nor blankets. Food was in such short supply that the soldiers were close to starving. They built themselves log huts, but the icy winter wind ripped through the cracks between the logs. Smoke from the hastily built fireplaces filled the huts. Much of the time they ate flour and water baked in thin cakes. "Fire-cake and water for breakfast," one of them cried. "Fire-cake and water for dinner. Fire-cake for supper. The Lord said that our Commissary for Purchases has to live on fire-cake and water."

Inevitably, there was much serious illness in the camp—smallpox, typhus, and other diseases raged. Physicians of the time could do little to cure such diseases, and men died in misery from them. These were times, as Thomas Paine had written, "that try men's souls. The summer soldier and the sunshine patriot will, in this crisis, shrink from the service of their country; but he that stands it *now* deserves the love and thanks of man and woman." Paine was right, for now, a year after he penned these words, a good many men proved to be summer soldiers, and deserted; but most stood firm. In the end, Washington, with the help of General Nathaniel Greene, managed to scour enough food from the countryside to keep the troops going, and when spring 1778 came the small army was again growing robust.

The contribution of American women to keeping the army going was considerable. As with the men, many ignored the war if they could, and others were Tories. But a great many joined in the fray. At the time, women legally were virtually the property of their husbands. They could not vote, and if they owned any property, it was their husbands' to do with as they liked. While it is true that most women had more than enough to do taking care of their children, their houses, and the family farm, working from daybreak to sunset and beyond, even those well-to-do women who had servants could not aspire to professional careers.

The laws which so enclosed women were of course colonial laws based on British models. Although most Americans took the system for granted, some women hoped that the new freedom for which the Americans were fighting would be extended to women. Abigail Adams strongly urged her husband to improve the position of women. She wrote him, "In the new code of laws which I suppose it will be necessary for you to make I desire you would remember the ladies, and be more generous and favorable to them than your ancestors." But, of course, no one paid any attention to her plea.

A few women actually managed to get into the fighting. The most famous of these was Mary Hays, today celebrated as Molly Pitcher. During the fighting in Manhattan in the first days, she fought beside her husband, John Corbin, a private in the artillery, helping him to load the cannon. He was killed during the battle, and she took over for him, firing the cannon herself. Finally she was hit by grapeshot, and one arm permanently disabled. After the war she was given a pension.

Other women joined their husbands in battle, and some enlisted disguised as men. But these were relatively few. Hundreds actually traveled with the army cooking and laundering for their husbands and their messmates. More often women aided the rebel cause by passing on information they picked up one way or another. During the British occupation of Philadelphia, some British officers staying at the home of Lydia Darrah began to discuss military matters. Darrah pretended to go to bed, but crept back, and listening at the door, discovered that the British were planning an attack on nearby Whitemarsh. In the morning she left home on the excuse that she needed to go to a mill for flour. The mill was not far from Whitemarsh. She got permission to pass through British lines, left her flour sack off at the mill, and then walked five miles through the snow to the American camp, where she reported what she had heard. When the British came out to attack Whitmarsh, the Americans were prepared, and the British hastily retreated.

Despite the brave deeds of women like Molly Pitcher and Lydia Darrah, the largest contribution made by American women to the rebel cause was to keep the farms and workshops going while their husbands, sons, and fathers were off fighting—or among the dead or wounded. Getting food for the soldiers was a terrible and everlasting problem for

Washington that was never really solved. The nation was dependent upon women to plant corn, milk cows, harvest apples, make cheese and butter, and bake bread. The war could not be fought by starving men, and it was the heroism of tens of thousands of forgotten women who kept the farms going with only the help of their children that made American victory possible.

But despite the improvement to the American army in the spring of 1778, Washington was in a difficult situation. Howe, to be sure, was still dallying in Philadelphia. It is difficult to understand him, for he had been courageous at Bunker Hill, where he had personally led his troops into the withering fire from the redoubt, and he had shown great skill in beating Washington on Long Island. But for some reason he was too often unwilling to exert himself when exertion was just what was called for. Howe's indecision or indolence would shortly prove to be a major weapon for the Americans.

Washington's problem lay elsewhere. Before the American defeats at Brandywine and Germantown, another British general, "Gentleman Johnny" Burgoyne, had worked out a plan that might finish the Americans off. Burgoyne's idea was that a relatively small force under Colonel Barry Saint Leger would move eastward toward Albany from Fort Oswego on Lake Ontario. General Howe would bring his army up the Hudson to Albany. Burgoyne, himself with a large force, would come down from Canada via the "water route"—Lake Champlain and Lake George. The three forces would take Albany, destroy any American army that dared oppose them, and clear the Hudson of Americans. This would effectively cut the New England colonies off from the rest, and the British could then take the colonies one by one at their leisure.

It was a good plan, but like so many good plans it went astray. Saint Leger started off as planned with a combination of British troops, Indians, and Loyalists willing to fight for their king. He was opposed by an American force under Benedict Arnold, known to history as a traitor

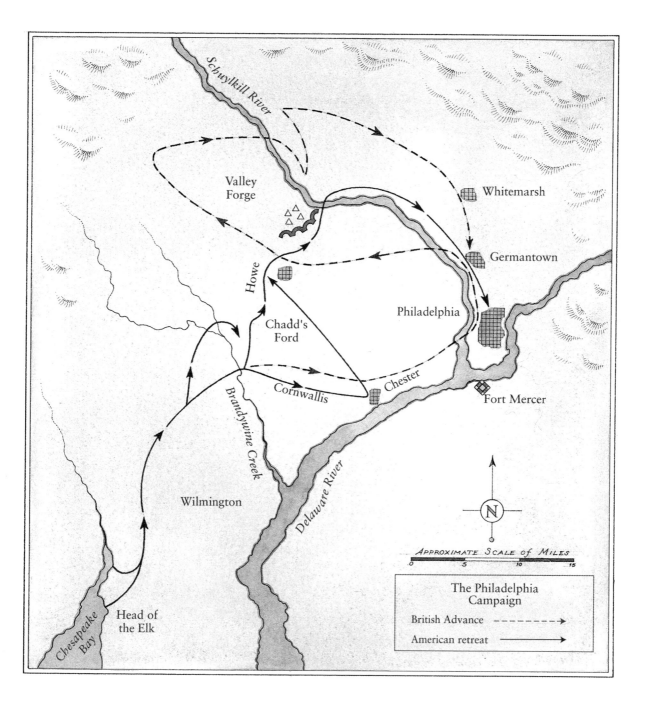

Valley Forge

Schuylkill River

Whitemarsh

Germantown

Howe

Philadelphia

Chadd's Ford

Cornwallis

Chester

Fort Mercer

Brandywine Creek

Wilmington

Delaware River

Head of the Elk

Chesapeake Bay

N

APPROXIMATE SCALE of MILES

0   5   10   15

The Philadelphia Campaign

British Advance ---------▶

American retreat ————▶

to the American cause, but in fact, one of the most brilliant generals in Washington's army. Americans put up effective resistance to Saint Leger's forces at Oriskany and Fort Stanwick. Through a ruse, Arnold left the impression with the British that he had a huge army in front of them. The Indians were taken in by the deception, and bolted for safety. The Loyalists, seeing the Indians depart, took leave themselves. Saint Leger no longer had a force sufficient for the job ahead of him, and was forced to retreat to Fort Oswego.

Meanwhile, General Howe, having defeated Washington at Brandywine, was sitting around Philadelphia enjoying himself. Although Burgoyne was counting on his help, Howe never made a move to leave the comforts of the city. Hapless Burgoyne, all unknowing that both of the other forces he was counting on would not be coming, set off for Albany.

The threat of British occupation, aided by their Indian allies, aroused the local farmers, and they joined in the fight, swelling the American forces. Burgoyne made it down from Canada by the water route as planned. At Bennington, in what is now Vermont, a contingent of his forces was attacked by the Green Mountain Boys, as they called themselves, under John Stark and badly mauled. Threatened by other American forces from the south and west, Burgoyne retreated to a high point near Saratoga Springs, New York, where Schuylerville is today.

For once the British were outnumbered. The American forces surrounded Burgoyne's high point on three sides, and began pouring in cannon fire. Burgoyne consulted with his generals, and it was decided to slip out through the open north side of the encampment while the going was good. All was in readiness, when Burgoyne changed his mind and canceled the retreat. He saw too late that the Americans had slipped in behind him and his retreat was cut off. They continued to pour cannon fire into the British encampment. Small detachments of Americans crept in where they could and picked away at the British with rifles. One of the British generals later wrote:

. . . the ground was covered with dead horses. . . . Even for the wounded no spot could be found which could afford them a safe shelter. . . . The whole camp was now a scene of constant fighting. The soldier could not lay down his arms day or night, except to exchange his gun for the space when new entrenchments were thrown up. The sick and wounded would drag themselves along into a quiet corner of the woods and lie down to die on the damp ground.

It was hopeless, and the British knew it. In the end, October 17, 1777, Burgoyne had no choice but to surrender.

An artist's idea of the surrender of the British General Burgoyne to the American General Gates at Saratoga in 1777. The battle was a turning point in the Revolution, for it showed that the Americans might win after all and encouraged the French to provide them with critically important aid.

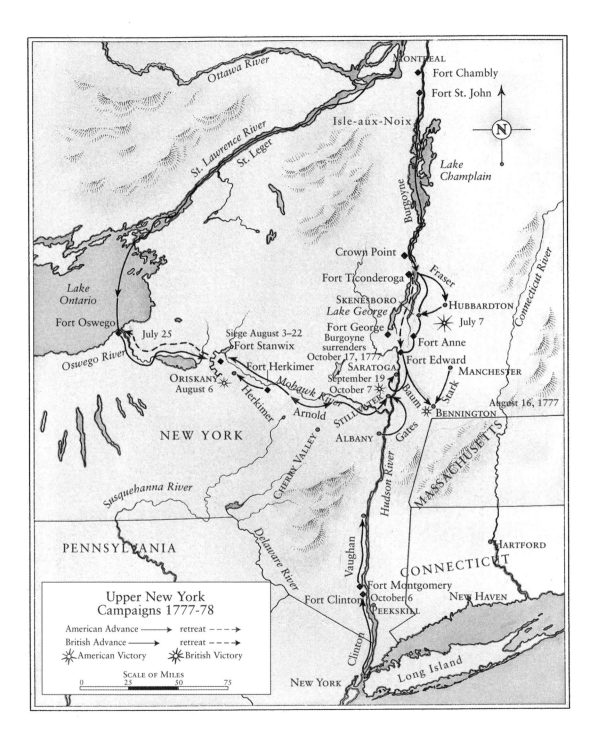

Ottawa River

St. Lawrence River

St. Leger

MONTREAL

Fort Chambly

Fort St. John

Isle-aux-Noix

N

Lake
Champlain

Burgoyne

Lake
Ontario

I.

Crown Point

Fort Ticonderoga

Fraser

Fort Oswego

July 25

SKENESBORO
Lake George

Fort George
Burgoyne
surrenders
October 17, 1777

HUBBARDTON

July 7

Siege August 3–22
Fort Stanwix

Fort Herkimer

Fort Anne

Fort Edward

ORISKANY
August 6

SARATOGA
September 19
October 7

Baum

MANCHESTER

Oswego River

Herkimer

Mobawk River

Stark

Arnold

STILLWATER

BENNINGTON

August 16, 1777

NEW YORK

Albany

Gates

CHERRY VALLEY

Susquehanna River

MASSACHUSETTS

PENNSYLVANIA

Delaware River

Hudson River

Vaughan

HARTFORD

CONNECTICUT

Fort Montgomery

October 6

NEW HAVEN

Fort Clinton

PEEKSKILL

Clinton

Upper New York
Campaigns 1777-78

American Advance ——→ retreat - - -→
British Advance ——→ retreat - - -→
✳ American Victory ✳ British Victory

SCALE OF MILES

0   25   50   75

NEW YORK

Long Island

Connecticut River

The American victory at Saratoga was the turning point in the war. It ended the British scheme to isolate New England from its sister colonies. Perhaps more important, it signaled to European nations that the Americans might actually win their freedom. This was something the European nations hoped for, not so much because of any love of liberty, but because the loss of the colonies would be a blow to England, rapidly becoming one of the dominant world powers.

The French had for some time been secretly supplying the Americans. Particularly important was America's minister to France, Benjamin Franklin. The wise and wily Franklin was extremely popular with the French and the French court, and had helped to gain sympathy in Paris for the American cause. But the French already had plenty of reason for wanting the English discomfited, for only fifteen years earlier the English had defeated them in America, and taken over the French colony of Canada.

Now, with the victory at Saratoga, the French decided to come in openly on the American side. The government recognized American independence, and in February 1778, France and America signed military and political treaties. France and England were now once again at war. The British, thoroughly alarmed, sent an emissary to America, offering to put everything back to where it had been in 1763 at the close of the French and Indian War. But it was too late: The Americans smelled victory, and rejected the offer. The war would be fought to the end. In 1779, Spain too came in against the British, and the next year the English went to war with the Dutch to cut off their trade with America.

The French now sent troops to America, and lent the country a great deal of money. As important as were Frenchmen, money, and matériel, equally so was its powerful navy. The Americans had long been building excellent ships in large quantities, and did have some gunships capable of giving the British a fight. But as a whole the British navy was far too powerful for the Americans to contend with. The British could fairly easily

Many young European officers rushed to America to get in on the excitement. Many of them demanded high posts and special treatment and were simply a nuisance to Washington. But a few of them were extremely helpful, like Baron von Steuben and the Marquis de Lafayette. Lafayette is shown here.

control American ports, although ships did slip through.

Now, with the French on their side, the Americans had a fleet capable of countering the British. And the French fleet would prove critical to what followed. After the enthusiasm following the victory at Saratoga, American spirits had sagged. The war had been going on too long. Soldiers frequently went unpaid, sometimes went hungry, and were always badly clothed. They deserted, and on eleven occasions mutinied against their officers. Yet somehow George Washington again and again suppressed the mutinies and rallied his men.

Nevertheless, neither side was able to close for the kill. The British, preoccupied with fighting in Europe, could not concentrate on the American war, and for the moment diverted their efforts. For the next two years fighting was desultory and inconclusive.

By 1780, the British had moved their military focus to the South. Once again the Americans suffered serious losses; at Charleston and again at Camden in South Carolina as they struggled to hold the wealthy but more vulnerable South. Very quickly the British gained control of South Carolina and Georgia. They started to move northward into North Carolina, but now the Americans stood firm, beating the English at King's Mountain, Cowpens, and again at Guilford Courthouse. General Cornwallis, the British officer in charge of the southern fighting, gave up on North Carolina and fought his way to Yorktown, Virginia.

In 1781, however, Cornwallis found himself in a precarious position. Washington had gathered a substantial force of over eight thousand troops, and he had with him his French allies who had seventy-eight hundred troops, all better trained and better equipped than the Americans. Cornwallis had fewer than eight thousand, but he had the advantage of terrain. Yorktown was on a bluff on the south side of the York River, which was only about a half mile wide at this point. Furthermore, deep ravines in the rear of the town gave him some protection from that direction. He could

In this reenactment at Yorktown, two American soldiers fire their muskets.

hold out for a while; and he assumed that shortly the British fleet, with more soldiers to reinforce him, would sail up the York River and save him.

What Cornwallis did not know was that the French fleet, under Admiral François Comte de Grasse, was on its way to Yorktown. De Grasse met some of the British ships coming to relieve Cornwallis at York and defeated them. Then he swept into Chesapeake Bay, and thus shoved the cork into the bottle. Cornwallis was trapped.

There is a wonderful story about George Washington, when he learned that de Grasse had got to Chesapeake before the British. According to one of Washington's biographers, a group of high French officers sailed down to the city of Chester to join Washington. As they came toward the town in their boat, "they described an amazing sight. A tall officer in blue and buff regimentals was jumping up and down, waving in one hand a hat and in the other a white handkerchief. Seen from the approaching boat, the dancing figure seemed to be His Excellency, General Washington, but, of course, that was impossible." But it was indeed the serious Washington jumping and shouting, "de Grasse, de Grasse." As one of the French officers put it, the noble Washington appeared like "a child whose every wish had been gratified." And, indeed, they had been.

Cornwallis knew he was beaten, but he was stubborn and resourceful. For days he held the Americans off, forcing them to take his outposts and redoubts one at a time with fierce hand-to-hand fighting. But the Americans and French bombarded him with cannon fire morning, noon, and night, silencing his own guns and blowing apart the town. On the morning of October 17, 1781, a drummer in a red coat appeared on the parapet and sounded a beat calling for a conference. In the roar of the cannons nobody could hear him, but they could see him well enough. The firing ceased. Cornwallis sent an officer out to meet with Washington, and within a few hours it was all over. The next day the British troops marched out of Yorktown, their bands playing an old British march called "The World Turned Upside Down."

In the Battle of Yorktown, the American and French forces captured or killed half the British troops in America. The rest of the king's army was bottled up in New York, and was not strong enough to do anything very aggressive against the Americans. The British were also fighting against the French, Spanish, and Dutch in the West Indies, where they had very lucrative island colonies. With the French fleet on their side, it was clear that Americans would now be hard for the British to beat. When word of Yorktown reached Lord North in London, he could do nothing but pace back and forth crying wildly, "Oh God, it is all over." And it was.

Why were the Americans able, finally, to beat what had been considered the mightiest army in the world, supported by a great navy? For one, there was General Howe's slowness to take action at the beginning. Had he pushed hard at Washington in that first terrible winter, he might well have destroyed the American army and captured Washington. Instead, he let Washington drive him out of New Jersey at Trenton, and for the British a great opportunity was lost.

For another, the general situation was ultimately favorable to the Americans. The British might beat the Americans as they did on Long Island, at Brandywine, and many other places; but Washington was always able somehow to find more men, more equipment, more courage. The British were always squeezing a balloon that would pop up at another place.

Finally, the help of the French was critical. Loans of money, beginning even before the Battle of Saratoga in 1777, and matériel gave the Americans a chance. And French aid after Saratoga entirely changed the odds. Without de Grasse's fleet to bottle up the British at Yorktown, Cornwallis would have been eventually rescued by British ships, and gone on fighting.

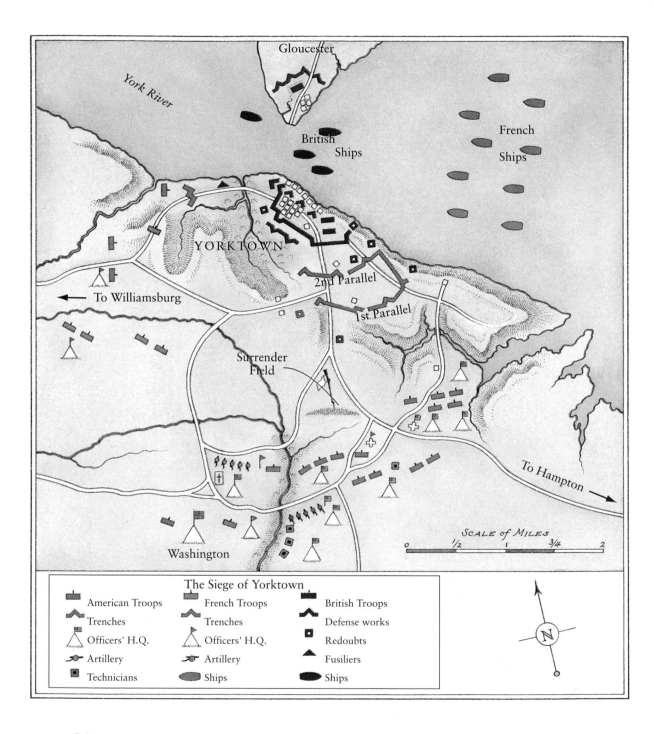

The Siege of Yorktown

American Troops	French Troops	British Troops
Trenches	Trenches	Defense works
Officers' H.Q.	Officers' H.Q.	Redoubts
Artillery	Artillery	Fusiliers
Technicians	Ships	Ships

Additionally, the British public had grown disheartened. The war appeared to go on endlessly, with the Americans showing admirable courage and determination. Some among the English public and politicians had never favored it in the first place; by the time of Yorktown, many were fed up with paying for a war that seemed to have no end, and could not very well be justified in any case. Increasingly, from 1778 on, public opinion was in favor of calling it quits and getting out.

Finally, there was the person of George Washington. Historians are generally agreed that without Washington the war could not have been

The surrender at Yorktown, rendered in a fine print that appeared in France. The town is center rear, and the French fleet bottling up the British army swarms in the river.

won. It is not that he was a great general; he was certainly a good one, and became better with experience, but he was not a military genius. Nor was he a great diplomat, like Benjamin Franklin, nor a master of finance, although he was certainly very intelligent.

What mattered about Washington was his character. He was, for one thing, utterly fearless in battle, again and again putting himself directly under fire to direct his men. For another, he was incorruptible: not only did he take no salary for himself during the war, he also made sure to turn in exact expense accounts, down to the last penny. He was a brilliant politician, able to keep thirteen bickering states working together. Beyond this, he was completely dedicated to the cause of his country. However disheartened he may have been at the time, he was inalterably determined to fight on, never to give in. And in the end, he found ways to win. Americans can be proud of many heroes; but we see George Washington as the greatest of them, because he was, put simply, truly heroic.

Although the war was effectively over after Yorktown, it took some time for the peace treaty to be ironed out. Negotiations took place in Paris, with John Adams, Benjamin Franklin, John Jay, and Henry Laurens acting for the Americans. Not until late in 1782 was a preliminary agreement reached, and signing did not take place until September 3, 1783.

The new United States came out of it very well. Independence was recognized by all parties. On the north, the present boundary with Canada was set. The western boundary was to be the Mississippi River, with what is now Florida and portions of Alabama and Mississippi ultimately going to Spain, France's ally during the war. Congress, without power to do more, could only urge the states to forgive Loyalists and give them their property back; and debts by all citizens of all countries would be honored, provisions that were found ultimately impossible to enforce.

So it was over. The colonies were at last free. Now they would see if they could turn themselves into a nation.

BIBLIOGRAPHY

Many of the books that are no longer in print may still be found in school or public libraries.

For Students

Brenner, Barbara. *If You Were There in 1776*. New York: Bradbury Press, 1994.

Chant, Christopher. *The Military History of the United States: The Revolutionary War*. Vol. 1. Tarrytown, N.Y. Marshall Cavendish

Dolan, Edward F. *The American Revolution: How We Fought the War of Independence*. Brookfield, Conn.: Millbrook Press, 1995.

Johnson, Neil. *The Battle of Lexington and Concord. New York:* Four Winds Press, 1992. (Out of print.)

Meltzer, Milton, ed. *The American Revolutionaries: A History in Their Own Words, 1750–1800*. New York: Thomas Y. Crowell, 1987.

For Teachers

Alden, John R. *The American Revolution.* New York: Harper and Row, 1954.

Billias, George A. *George Washington's Generals.* New York: William Morrow, 1964.

_____. *George Washington's Opponents.* New York: William Morrow, 1969.

Fischer, David Hackett. *Paul Revere's Ride.* New York: Oxford University Press, 1994.

Gipson, Lawrence H. *The Coming of the American Revolution, 1763–1775.* New York: Harper and Row, 1954. (Out of print.)

Higginbotham, Don. *The War of American Independence.* New York: Macmillan, 1971.

Labaree, Benjamin W. *The Boston Tea Party.* New York: Oxford University Press, 1964.

Wood, Gordon S. *The Creation of the American Republic, 1776–1787.* Chapel Hill: University of North Carolina Press, 1969.

Zobel, Hiller B. *The Boston Massacre.* New York: W. W. Norton, 1970.

INDEX

JAMES LINCOLN COLLIER is the author of a number of books both for adults and for young people, including the social history *The Rise of Selfishness in America*. He is also noted for his biographies and historical studies in the field of jazz. Together with his brother, Christopher Collier, he has written a series of award-winning historical novels for children widely used in schools, including the Newbery Honor classic, *My Brother Sam Is Dead*. A graduate of Hamilton College, he lives with his wife in New York City.

CHRISTOPHER COLLIER grew up in Fairfield County, Connecticut and attended public schools there. He graduated from Clark University in Worcester, Massachusetts and earned M.A. and Ph.D. degrees at Columbia University in New York City. After service in the Army and teaching in secondary schools for several years, Mr. Collier began teaching college in 1961. He is now Professor of History at the University of Connecticut and Connecticut State Historian. Mr. Collier has published many scholarly and popular books and articles about Connecticut and American history. With his brother, James, he is the author of nine historical novels for young adults, the best known of which is *My Brother Sam Is Dead*. He lives with his wife Bonnie, a librarian, in Orange, Connecticut.